I Found a So

Written by Vic Parker
Illustrated by Sarah Horne

Collins

Tick-tock! It is my clock.
The bell rings and I get up.

2

Pop! It is my toast.
I like it with lots of jam.

Out and about, cars zoom.
Trucks clank and trains chug.

Bash, toot, boom! It is a band!
Mum sings, and Dad and I clap.

In the park, a flag flaps.
I step on sticks that snap.

6

A man and his dog jog.
He huffs and puffs. The dog pants.

We munch and crunch our lunch.
Fizz, gulp! I swig my drink.

At the bin, bees buzz and flies hum.
Crash! I drop in the rubbish.

Pit-pat! It is the rain.
Squelch! I stomp in mud.

Croak! It is a toad at the pond.
Plop! He hops in for a swim.

Hiss! Mum grills fish.
Bash! Mum cooks mash.
Glug! Dad puts pans in the sink
to soak.

Hush! I need to sleep.

Sounds of my day

tick-tock!

pop!

toot!

hush!

hiss!

snap!

fizz!

plop!

squelch!

crash!

15

Ideas for reading

Written by Clare Dowdall, PhD
Lecturer and Primary Literacy Consultant

Learning objectives: read simple words by sounding out and blending the phonemes all through the word from left to right; read a range of familiar and common words and simple sentences independently; show an understanding of how information can be found in non-fiction texts to answer questions; extend their vocabulary, exploring the meanings and sounds of new words; use talk to organise, sequence and clarify thinking, ideas, feelings and events, exploring the meanings and sounds of new words

Curriculum links: Creative Development: Creating music and dance; Knowledge and Understanding of the World: Exploration and investigation

Focus phonemes: ou, oa, oo, ai, ch, ee, zz

Fast words: I, my, the, like, he, we

Word count: 148

Getting started

- Read the title on the front cover. Look at the words *found* and *sound*. Ask children to suggest other words with the *ou* phoneme.

- Revise the focus phonemes *oo* and *oa*. Ask children to skim through pp2–5 to find and read words containing these phonemes.

- Revise the focus phoneme *zz*. Ask children to suggest sound words that contain this phoneme, e.g. buzz.

- Ask children to predict the sounds that the boy might hear in the rest of the book.

Reading and responding

- Ask children to read the book from the beginning, using their phonics skills to sound out each word.

- Move around the group, praising blending and accurate sounding out of new words with long vowel phonemes, e.g. *toast, zoom, train*.

- Encourage children to reread sentences fluently following sounding out.

- Invite fast finishers to reread the book, collecting sound words by writing them on a whiteboard.